## VISION ACCELERATOR

A STEP BY STEP TOOLKIT TO TRANSFORM
YOUR GOALS INTO REALITY

ABHISHEK SHARMA

www.shakethecosmos.com

*To my mom,*
*Vijay, and her profound lessons*

# VISION ACCELERATOR
# THE SHAKE THE COSMOS EXPERIENCE!

Dear Friend,

Welcome, and congratulations on starting your journey forward toward lasting success and fulfillment in your career and your life.

Unlike other personal development workbooks, *Shake the Cosmos Vision Accelerator* is an immersive experience featuring goal-setting strategies that will last for decades. Your journey will include unlocking and accelerating your vision and calling and bringing your goals to the forefront. By transforming how you think about vision, love, purpose, and action, you can create a life in which you are doing the things you enjoy—the life that you desire and deserve.

Get ready to take a full plunge into finding your true calling, supercharging your support systems, and taking charge of your goals.

Thank you for joining me on this journey.

Shake the Cosmos!

**ABHISHEK SHARMA**

# PRAISE FOR SHAKE THE COSMOS VISION ACCELERATOR

## From Kundalini Yoga Community

***The title of this book,* Shake the Cosmos*, meaning taking action for massive transformation is totally appropriate. Abhishek has done a great job of packing the book with actionable techniques that he has taught all over the world. This is a go-to-handbook for goal-setting.***

**Meherbani Kaur**, is Kundalini Research Institute (KRI) Lead Kundalini Yoga teacher trainer and mentor. She has practiced and taught Kundalini Yoga most of her adult life and teaches from her heart with simplicity and humor. In addition to Kundalini Yoga, she also practices and teaches healing art of Sat Nam Rasayan®. She is one of a handful of practitioners worldwide who have been designated to teach this sacred art. In 2016, she and the 3HO community opened Cosmic Flow Kundalini Yoga studio. www.cosmicflowyoga.com.

***This is a great workbook that Abhishek has created to help people understand and achieve their goals. All the different techniques he offers for people to use: breathing, journaling, feeling, moving, dancing, meditation and more, allow individuals to become aware and clear about how to move themselves in the right direction, feeling safe and supported and ultimately to live feeling fulfilled.***

**Simran Kaur**, second-generation Yogi (daughter of the SatJivan's NYC), and wife and teaching partner of Posture Master GuruPrem Singh. She has dedicated herself to teaching, inspiring and being an example of people who live a Vibrant, Active, Calm, Happy, Flexible & Fun life! She has taught the techniques in the books *Divine Alignment & The Heart Rules* in relationship to being in a body, any Activity one does & Kundalini Yoga. She studied in India for 10 years, Mastered Bound Lotus Kriya, teaches in Teacher Training all over the world. https://www.yogawithsimran.com/

# PRAISE FOR SHAKE THE COSMOS VISION ACCELERATOR

*I was going through a tough time professionally.* Shake the Cosmos *helped me mentally set up game plans and kept me accountable to stick with them, which led me to find a much more rewarding career with a better work-life balance.*

Jon, California, USA

*I had an incredible experience with* Shake the Cosmos*! I found the course easy to follow, but it provided profound transformational vision techniques. We completed our own booklets throughout the seminar, which also included celebratory dance parties after we completed each step, which I believed harnessed the power of Law of Attraction. Just one month after completing the seminar, I quit my job and launched my own business. I also walked my partner through the booklet as well and he is on his way to doing the same. I can't thank Abhishek and this program enough!! Thank you thank you!*

Kimberly, California, USA

*I would highly recommend this workbook! It will inspire, motivate, and ground you at the same time. If you are going through a confusing time or need some direction about what your life purpose is, this course will provide that first step towards helping to identify what you really want and how to get it! Abhishek is very gifted and he holds space for the group with such ease, facilitating a very natural flow to the whole experience.*

Ela, California, USA

*I enjoyed the simple, reflective, and actionable steps included in the program. It is important to prioritize time to assess your goals and what is meaningful to you, and these activities did just that for me. A great way to reconnect with your purpose and create momentum toward living in it.*

Dudney, Massachusetts, USA

# FOREWORD

# DARREN REINKE

Purpose. It's a word and concept that seems unachievable to most people. Purpose is reserved for those people featured in TED Talks and *New York Times* best-selling books who found purpose seemingly in a flash. Or so I thought.

As the son of two veterinarians, I also thought I would explore a career in health science. The plan was to go to medical school after my undergrad years at UC Davis and eventually become an orthopedic surgeon. I looked forward to a job that could help people by alleviating their pain and enabling them to get back out doing what they loved. So, in my junior year in college, I volunteered in the ER at the UC Davis Medical Center in Sacramento. I was exposed to life-threatening emergencies and surgeons working their magic to keep people alive. I was inspired by their ability to help people, but the idea of working in the same trade year after year and toiling in a sterile hospital environment lost its appeal. I realized that medicine wasn't the path for me.

At the same time, I was taking a few general education business classes and I became intrigued by what I considered the nebulous world of business. Luckily for me, my best friend's dad was a high-level executive at a large bank and offered to mentor me. He encouraged me to go work for a consulting firm or investment bank so that I "could figure things out." It was great advice, and working for Accenture prior to receiving my MBA gave me a business foundation that has been instrumental throughout my career.

Since my mid-college career pivot, I have spent the majority of my career seeking a sense of fulfillment and meaning, something I now fully grasp is my purpose. I put in my time as a management consultant at Accenture and spent time working for companies with household names such as Gap, Neutrogena, and FTD (formerly ProFlowers). At each of those stops, I learned about marketing, strategy, and building processes, while helping each of them achieve their own goals. I was intellectually challenged, earned a steady paycheck, and worked with some incredibly smart people. But something was missing.

Several years ago, a friend and mentor told me about a coach training program she had signed up for. As a former high school athlete, I knew of coaching in a sports context. But coaching in a business context? I was intrigued and I signed up for a six-day accelerated executive coaching training program. For once in my life, I started something not knowing what the outcome would be. For me, it was the start of a meaningful career as an executive coach, author, speaker, and corporate trainer. My new career has allowed me to deliver on my desire to help people, but in a business context. I had finally found my purpose: *To help unleash the inner lion within leaders so that they can lead more authentic and joyful lives while creating stronger and more resilient teams, organizations, and communities*. It led me to launch Group Sixty, an executive coaching and training company and to write my first book, *The Savage Leader: 13 Principles to Become a Better Leader from the Inside Out*.

Yes, I had found my purpose, but it took me almost 20 years to do so. I wish I had found a book and course like Shake the Cosmos earlier in my career as it surely would have accelerated my path to find meaning and purpose. This book will help you take the first step to figuring out what inspires you and matters most so that you can find fulfillment and meaning in your career and life. Lean in and commit to a better and more joyful YOU. Shake the Cosmos!

Best,
Darren Reinke

*Darren Reinke is an executive coach and author with a different take on leadership. Darren focuses on the internal journey, which is often overlooked.*

# HOW TO USE THIS WORKBOOK

This book is divided into five chapters:

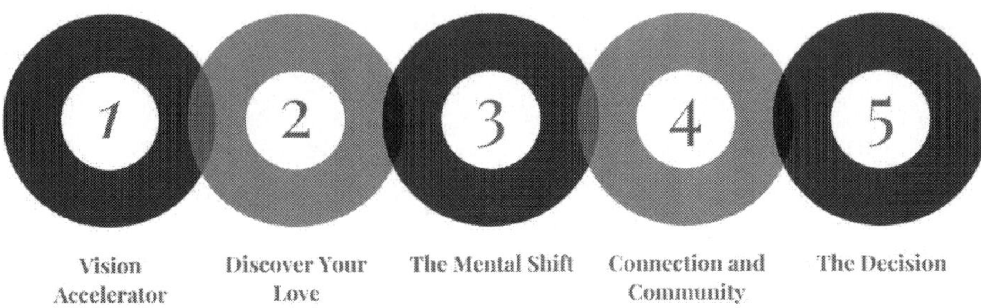


**Journaling:** Each chapter has a set of journaling exercises that are self-paced, so feel free to pause and take as much time needed to self-reflect. If you hit a roadblock, see if you can understand where the resistance is coming from. For each question, the recommended time is given.

**Rapid Journaling**: There is some recommended "rapid journaling" as well. When you see the following icon , write only for 2-3 minutes. Rapid journaling allows you to write your thoughts down on paper without too much filtering.

**Discussion Prompts:** If you are using this workbook as part of a group, or with a friend or partner, there are discussion points identified by the icon. You can take a few minutes to share your responses.

**Guided "Bonus" Meditations:** There are several meditations given throughout the book. The meditations train the neutral mind so you can be focused and most productive in the exercises.

# THE PROMISE
# A COMMITMENT TO YOURSELF

Before you begin, it's time to make a promise and commitment to yourself.

Write your name and date below and read out loud the promise that you are making yourself as you start this workbook.

I, ______________________, am making the following three commitments as I complete this workbook:

I promise myself to keep an OPEN MIND. I understand the mind is like a parachute, and it works best when it's open.

I promise myself to participate and take the time to self-reflect in the activities. I understand that participating will maximize the results of the exercises.

I promise myself to BE SELFISH. I understand that this is really for me.

Name: ______________________

Date: ______________________

Let's get started!

# Contents

# CHAPTER 1.
# VISION ACCELERATOR

When I first moved to San Diego from Sacramento, people would ask me, "Why did you move here?"

I said there were philosophical reasons and career reasons behind the move. Guess which reasons people always wanted to know more about? Philosophical reasons, as those represented my true "why."

I had visited the city a few times for client meetings during my tenure as Product Manager at The Jackson Laboratory. I enjoyed the weather and the exciting med-tech scene. Whenever I was visiting clients in San Diego, or was there for any reason at all, I felt an indescribable feeling of attraction and love to the city.

So, today you are going to dive deeper into YOUR WHY using an activity known as the "vision accelerator" to unlock your focus and vision.

**OBJECTIVE:** Making a powerful transition from a state of planning to a state of living a fulfilling life and identifying what's truly important to you. Listening to that deep inner voice that informs you of your true purpose and vision so you are living a fulfilling life, and feeling that you are always doing the right thing, at the right place, at the right time.

**TIME REQUIRED:** 10 MINUTES

**PREP:** Start with a quick guided meditation.

**Guided Meditation on Focus, Clarity, and Vision Accelerator.**

1. Get comfortable, sitting in a chair or on the floor.

   a. Take a deep breath in through your nose and exhale through the mouth.
   b. Take another breath in through the nose and exhale through the mouth.
   c. Take another one with a sound, inhale through the nose and exhale through the mouth with the sound AHHHH.
2. Connecting with a moment in time.
   a. Can you remember a time when you felt:
      i. Totally **focused?**
      ii. Totally **empowered?**
      iii. Totally **supported?**
3. As you go back to that time now, float down into your body and see what you saw, hear what you heard, and **feel totally focused, feel totally empowered, and feel totally supported.**
4. Now, take a deep breath in through the nose and exhale through the mouth.

**TIP:** This workbook has blank spaces for the journal questions. Please feel free to use a notebook for your responses while reading. You can also download and print the chapter questions as a PDF at

www.shakethecosmos.com/resources

**VISION ACCELERATOR ACTIVITY:**

Imagine for a minute these three circles: "Future" on the far right, then "Present" in the middle, then an unnamed circle on the left. Take a look at the graphic below:

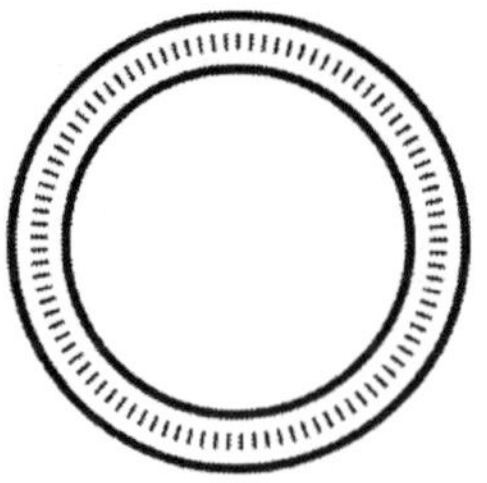

Now, take 2 minutes and jot down the answer to the following question.

- **WHAT ARE YOU PLANNING FOR YOUR FUTURE? Write down the things you are planning for 3 months from now, 6 months from now, 1 year from now, 5 years from now.**

What did you notice? Any trends or something that surprised you?

Now, move on to the second step.

PRESENT

FUTURE

Take a moment to remind yourself what day and time it is. For example, as I write this, it is September 9, 2021, at 2:00 pm.

Now, take 2 minutes and jot down the answer to the following question:

- **WHAT ARE SOME THINGS ON YOUR MIND TODAY, IN THE PRESENT MOMENT? For example, you are reading this book and following these instructions. What are you really feeling today?**

______________________________

______________________________

______________________________

______________________________

______________________________

______________________________

______________________________

______________________________

______________________________

______________________________

Thank you for completing this step. Now, on to the third step. But first . . .

Take a look back at the three circles. You might be wondering by now, what is that third blank circle? The third circle is the "CALLING."

CALLING PRESENT FUTURE

Calling is the inner voice to which we often say, "Shut Up!" It's the voice or calling deep inside of us that is always telling us what to do, but we tell it to be quiet.

For me, MY calling or inner voice was: move to San Diego. And guess what? When I followed my calling, things fell in place . . .

My real estate business took off and provided over 60% return to investors.

I found a dream job, and a dream boss, where I felt supported.

I found a yoga ashram and yoga training and realized that when I was growing up, countless scholarships and mentors had helped me.

So, I created a vision to give back and give back aggressively. Now my vision is to live a lifestyle in which, 10 years from now, I give back 50% of my income.

Ultimately, following my calling unlocked my vision, and it feels like I am doing the RIGHT THINGS, IN THE RIGHT PLACE, AT THE RIGHT TIME.

So, what about you?

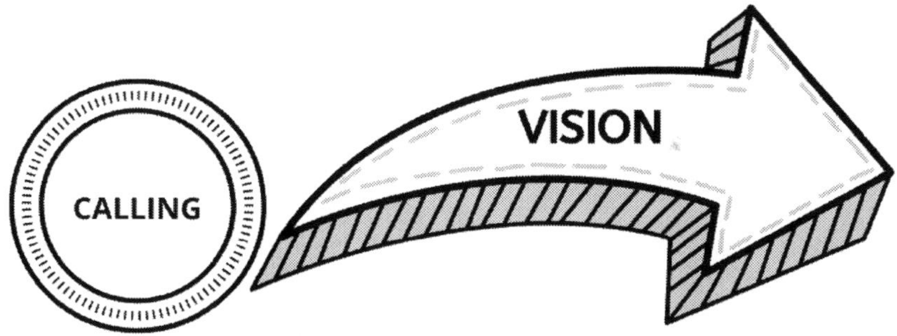


**Take 3 minutes to write down the answer to the following question:**

- **WHAT IS YOUR INNER VOICE OR CALLING TELLING YOU TODAY? This is an important step as, once you identify it, your calling forms a vision. This is your X-factor—the thing that sets you apart from the rest of the world.**

______________________________________________

______________________________________________

GREAT JOB. YOU DID IT! Now that your calling is on paper, it's more memorable, "focus-able," and "manifest-able."

**TAKEAWAY:** Is this your first time writing down what your inner voice is saying? There is power in writing things down; you may look back at this page a few months or years from now and see how what you wrote down became true.

Identifying your calling will soon become a differentiator in your life, business, personal relationships, and career.

**CELEBRATE:** This moment calls for celebration, doesn't it? There is nothing better than some dancing and moving the body to celebrate. Dancing yields a new state in your body, mind, and soul, so you are not only excited about this calling of yours, but you also are ready to take steps to put it into action.

Put on your favorite dance tunes . . . just dance and shake your hands, legs, and body, for 1 or 2 minutes as if you've just won a million dollars. Dance as if you have just sent that final email at work or finished that final assignment. You are now ready to rock your wings!

How was that? See you in Chapter 2, where **you'll discover and create a blueprint of the love you currently have in your life.**

# CHAPTER 2.

# DISCOVER YOUR LOVE AND PASSION

When I was 25, I met my first girlfriend through a dating website called OkCupid, and I remember how thankful I was that the website brought us together.

Ha! So, why am I mentioning this? Today, we'll focus on creating a blueprint of YOUR love and passion.

**OBJECTIVE:** Find what you love around you, in your work and beyond.

**TIME REQUIRED:** 15 minutes

**PREP:** Start with a quick guided meditation.

**Guided Meditation on Discovering Love and Passion.**

1. Get comfortable, sitting in a chair or on the floor.
   a. Take a deep breath in through your nose and exhale through the mouth.
   b. Take another breath in through the nose and exhale through the mouth.
   c. Take another one with a sound, inhale through the nose and exhale through the mouth with the sound AHHHH.
2. Connecting with a moment in time.
   a. Can you remember a time when you felt:
      i. Totally **loved?**
      ii. Totally **supported?**
      iii. Totally **fearless?**

3. As you go back to that time now, float down into your body and see what you saw, hear what you heard, and **feel totally loved, feel totally supported, and feel totally fearless.**
4. Now, take a deep breath in through the nose and exhale through the mouth.

**TIP:** This workbook has blank spaces for the journal questions. Please feel free to use a notebook for your responses while reading. You can also download and print the chapter questions as a PDF at

www.shakethecosmos.com/resources

**DISCOVER YOUR LOVE AND PASSION ACTIVITY:**

**Take 1 minute to jot down the answers to the following questions:**

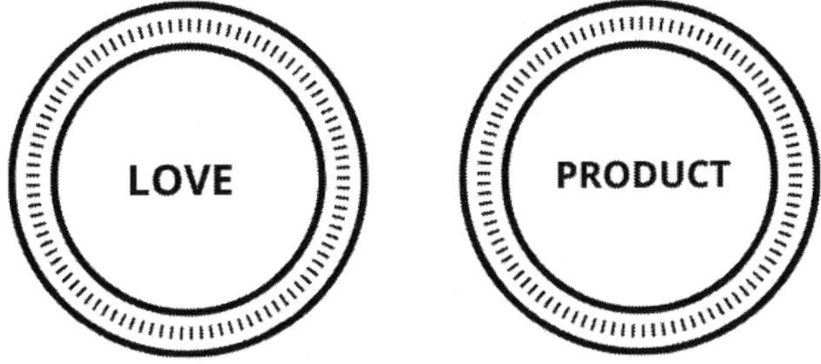


- **WHAT ARE SOME PRODUCT(S) THAT YOU LOVE OR ENJOY USING? For example, a website or app, a table, or that beautiful IKEA furniture, etc.**

_______________

_______________

_______________

_______________

_______________

_______________

_______________

---

---

Now, nice job on that. Take a moment to feel gratitude for having access to PRODUCTS that you love and enjoy.

Before you go into the next writing prompt, a quick little story . . .

I remember a time when I was unhappy at my job. I went to my boss and let him know that I was looking for another job. This is sort of a taboo—you are generally NOT supposed to tell your boss something like this.

My boss didn't flinch at all and said, "I'm sorry to hear that you will be leaving but I understand you're looking for something new. Let me know how I can help you. Maybe I can connect you with some people externally to make your search easier."

So, I was filled with gratitude for the support I was receiving at work.

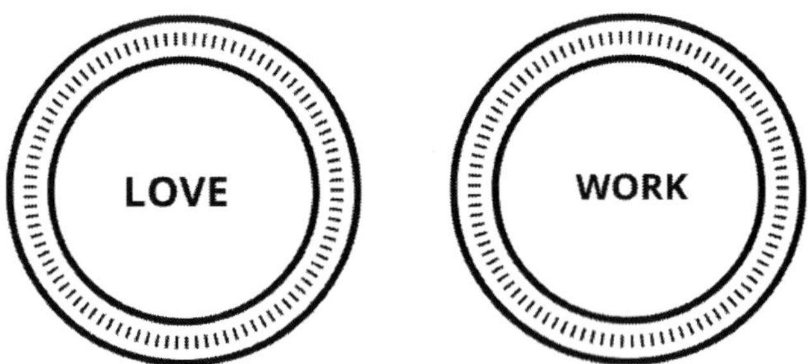


Now, your turn. Take 1 minute to jot down the answers to the following:

- **WHAT ARE SOME THINGS ABOUT YOUR WORK OR BUSINESS YOU LOVE OR ENJOY? For example, the carpet, parking, commuting, boss, etc. If you are currently a student, think of your school as your work or business as you answer this question.**

---

What trends are you seeing in the work things you enjoy? Maybe you really enjoy something that you have not noticed before?

Now, before going to the next prompt, another story . . .

Sometimes I like to visualize life as a four-legged coffee table. For me, one of the legs of this table is yoga. The technology of yoga is something that helps me stay focused and stable. If I don't do yoga during a particular week, I don't feel the same. It feels as if the table, or life, is lopsided. I am guessing you have activities that are similar, am I right? Something you do to maintain a sense of balance? Maybe you go to church every week, or do kick-boxing, or go running, etc.

So, your turn. Take 1 minute to jot down the answers to the following:

- **WHAT IS A TECHNOLOGY YOU LOVE OR ENJOY? SOMETHING THAT HAS CHANGED YOUR LIFE IN A BEAUTIFUL AND MEANINGFUL WAY? IT CAN BE ANYTHING THAT HELPS YOU ACCOMPLISH YOUR GOALS. For example, being able to text message, having the ability to travel by planes, doing yoga, etc.**

Look back now at your three lists: products you love, work you enjoy, and technologies you admire.

**TAKEAWAY:** What you have just accomplished is a blueprint of the products, the things at work, and the technologies you have access to TODAY. Feel that gratitude for these things in your life.

**CELEBRATE:** What's next? Well, you did well today, so, again, **put on your favorite dance tunes and move your body. Just move it as if you just had the most amazing food ever. Go wild with your moves for just 1 minute.**

And that's it. You are done with Chapter 2. Thanks for following through. In the next chapter, **we'll focus on creating a mental shift and you'll walk away with a new mindset toward achieving the things you really desire.**

Shaking the Cosmos yet?

# CHAPTER 3.

# THE MENTAL SHIFT TO GROWTH AND SUCCESS

**OBJECTIVE:** Making a mindset shift that's going to make your wants and dreams a reality.

**TIME REQUIRED:** 10 minutes

**PREP:** Start with a quick guided meditation.

**Guided Meditation on Making a Mental Shift**

1. Get comfortable, sitting in a chair or on the floor
   a. Take a deep breath in through your nose and exhale through the mouth.
   b. Take another breath in through the nose and exhale through the mouth.
   c. Take another one with a sound, inhale through the nose and exhale through the mouth with the sound AHHHH
2. Connecting with a moment in time.
   a. Can you remember a time when you felt:
      i. Totally **powerful?**
      ii. Totally **confident?**
      iii. Totally **creative?**
3. As you go back to that time now, float down into your body and see what you saw, hear what you heard, and **feel totally powerful, feel totally confident, and feel totally creative.**

4. Now, take a deep breath in through the nose and exhale through the mouth.

**TIP:** This workbook has blank spaces for the journal questions. Please feel free to use a notebook for your responses while reading. You can also download and print the chapter questions as a PDF at

www.shakethecosmos.com/resources

**MAKING A MENTAL SHIFT ACTIVITY:**

This one is going to be short and sweet. So, get out your journal, select some favorite tunes for background music, and **write down the following in the next 2-3 minutes. You can use the worksheet on the next page also.**

Your answers can be anything. Go wild. Heck, you can put down: I really want to be a MILLIONAIRE. I really want a beautiful, sexy partner. I really want a boyfriend / girlfriend or a dream job—whatever it may be.

## THE MENTAL SHIFT TO GROWTH AND SUCCESS

| |
|---|
| **1. I REALLY want . . .** |
| **2. I REALLY want . . .** |
| **3. I REALLY want . . .** |
| **4. I REALLY want . . .** |
| **5. I REALLY want . . .** |
| **6. I REALLY want . . .** |

When you are done writing your wish list, reflect on the following:

Growing up, my parents watched a lot of Discovery and National Geographic Channel. Full disclaimer, hopefully, nobody who is reading this works for PETA.

I remember watching shows where the tigers chased their prey, whether it was a buffalo or giraffe, and guess what happens after the tigers got their prey? It is game over for the prey; they are dead.

For a tiger, a predator, the prey is the dream, it's the "catch" – the thing they really desire. And, what happens at the end? It's dead.

We don't want the same result for our dreams. You don't want them to die, and that can happen if we have a "chase mindset." So, that's why in this next step, you are going to make a shift, a mental shift.

**Underneath each of your "I really want . . ." statements, write down, "I am . . ." or "I have . . ." So, for example, if you wrote, "I really want a dream job," then write down, "I have a dream job." Get the idea?**

So, take 2-3 minutes and write things down. You can use the same worksheet from the previous page. IMPORTANT: Save this list, as you will use it toward the end of the course.

Congratulations on making this shift! When I tried this exercise, I posted the new list on my bathroom mirror and read it out loud for 21 days. Many things started becoming true. Try it for yourself! :)

# CHAPTER 4.

# CONNECTION AND COMMUNITY

Are you ready for this? This is going to be phenomenal. Congrats and great job so far on following through.

**OBJECTIVE:** Create a blueprint of YOUR connections and community that you have today.

**TIME REQUIRED:** 8 minutes

**PREP:** Start with a quick guided meditation.

**Guided Meditation on Connection and Community:**

1. Get comfortable, sitting in a chair or on the floor
   a. Take a deep breath in through your nose and exhale through the mouth.
   b. Take another breath in through the nose and exhale through the mouth.
   c. Take another one with a sound, inhale through the nose and exhale through the mouth with the sound AHHHH
2. Connecting with a moment in time.
   a. Can you remember a time when you felt:
      i. Totally **connected?**
      ii. Totally **loved?**
      iii. Totally **amazing?**
3. As you go back to that time now, float down into your body and see what you saw, hear what you heard, and **feel totally connected, feel totally loved, and feel amazing.**
4. Now, take a deep breath in through the nose and exhale through the mouth.

**TIP:** This workbook has blank spaces for the journal questions. Please feel free to use a notebook for your responses while reading. You can also download and print the chapter questions as a PDF at

www.shakethecosmos.com/resources

## CONNECTION AND COMMUNITY ACTIVITY

One day, I asked myself, what's the most powerful force in the world? The answer for me, at the time, was nature, as it is a force that can end humankind at any time. What can we learn from nature? Well, nature is a supported system.

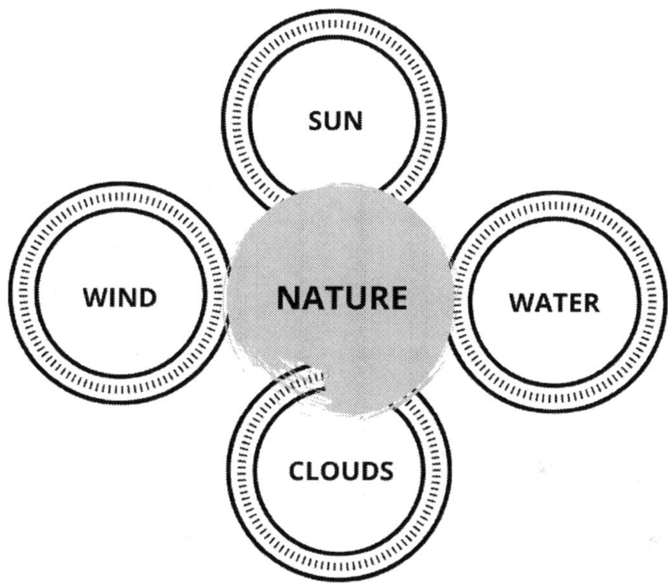


Nature has the Sun . . . providing warmth and heat, but it can also burn (ever get a sunburn?).

Nature has Water . . . it quenches our thirst and is flexible as it flows through obstacles, and it changes color; however, excess of it can also bring about floods.

Nature has Clouds . . . nurturing as it provides shade, but clouds can also bring torrential rains.

Nature has the Wind . . . it connects us all. You and I are breathing the same air, an invisible connection, but it can also cause destruction through tornadoes.

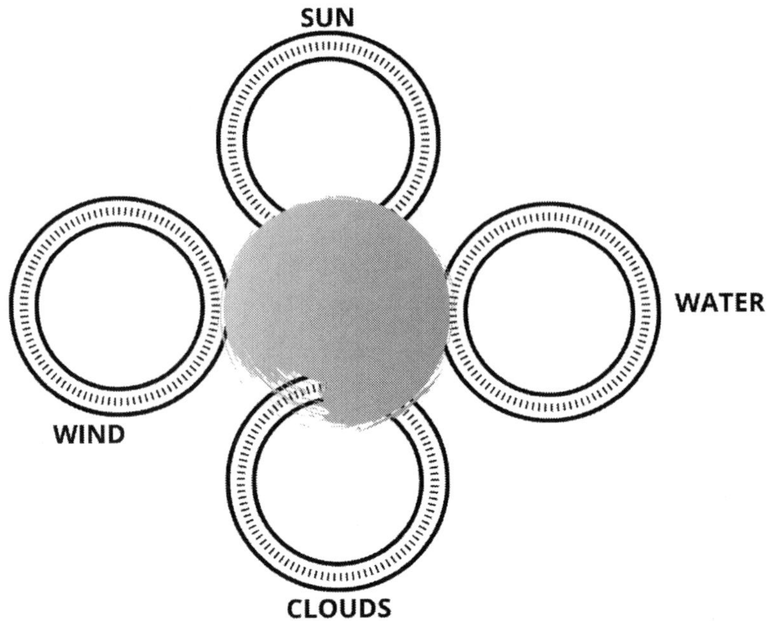


So, now what about YOU? **Take 3-4 minutes to jot down the following:**

- **WHO MAKES UP YOUR COMMUNITY? Your Sun, someone who helps you be bold? Your Water, a person who helps you be flexible? Your Cloud, a nurturer? Your Wind, a connector? For example, a mentor, a friend, a coworker, a boss, a parent, etc.**

**TAKEAWAY:** Now, looking back, you may see some sections where you do not have anyone or anything listed, and that's completely OK. They are opportunities for growth. This is a blueprint of your support system—the one you already have today; feel some gratitude for that.

**CELEBRATE:** And that is it for Chapter 4! **Put down your journal, turn on your favorite music, and celebrate that you have put your support system on paper today. Move that body and shake those limbs!**

In Chapter 5, the final chapter of the course, **you'll walk away with an actionable plan for a stronger, more peaceful, and fulfilled you.** Continuing Shaking the Cosmos!

# CHAPTER 5.

# DECISION AND COMMITMENT

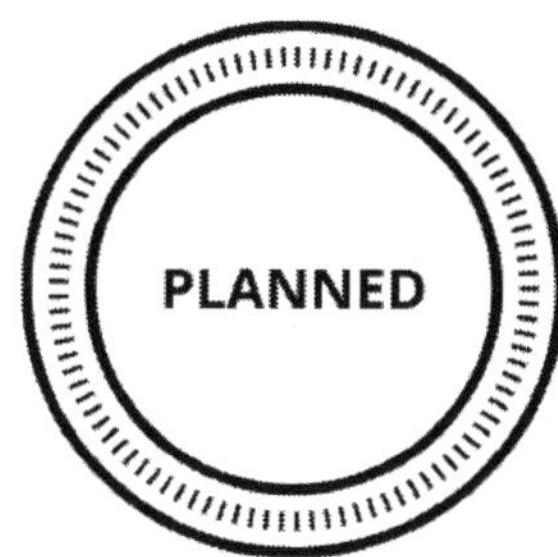


A few years ago, I was living in the United Arab Emirates (UAE) in the Middle East, and people asked what made me want to come to the UAE? I told them I just came to see the New Year's fireworks in Dubai, and the rest is history. That is, I made new friendships, created real estate ventures, fell in love (then fell out of love), and started teaching yoga full time at some of Middle East's best yoga studios. One random decision to come to the UAE, a country I knew very little about, led to so many opportunities.

So, sometimes random decisions can lead to random opportunities. Over 80% of people live in a world in which they plan their days and hope for planned outcomes.

I live in that world too. I got my MBA from UC-Berkeley Haas School of Business, which was a planned event. However, doing something random (like I have a reminder set to do every Sunday at 12:00 pm) can lead to random fulfilling opportunities.

**Take 2 minutes and write in your journal your answer to the following question:**

- **WHAT IS ONE RANDOM DECISION THAT HAS POSITIVELY SHAPED YOUR LIFE? HOW DID YOUR LIFE CHANGE FOR THE BETTER?**

________________________________________

________________________________________

________________________________________

________________________________________

________________________________________

________________________________________

________________________________________

________________________________________

________________________________________

________________________________________

Feel gratitude for that decision and the beauty it brought in your life.

**MAKING DECISION AND COMMITMENT ACTIVITY:**

Now, go back to your notes in Chapter 3 (The Mental Shift), where you made a list of things ("I really want . . ."). **Pick three things from that list and write them down.**

**So, it should look like this:**

1. I really want . . .
2. I really want . . .
3. I really want . . .

**But wait! Do you know what happens to goals without deadlines or timelines? They never become reality. So, this next step is very important.**

**Take a look at the three things you really want. Now, WHAT ARE**

**THREE NEW ACTIONS YOU CAN COMMIT TO MAKING TO EMPOWER YOUR VISION AND LIFE? WHEN WILL YOU TAKE THESE ACTIONS?**

For example, "I will visit the local museum and talk to the director about an intern position by September 2." "I will email the supervisor and set up a career development meeting by September 15." You get the idea, right?

| ACTION I WILL TAKE | DEADLINE |
| --- | --- |
| 1. I will . . . | |
| 2. I will . . . | |
| 3. I will . . . | |

**Now, take those three actions and write them in a place you can see them every day.**

**OK. YOU DID IT. YOU SHOOK THE COSMOS.**

**Now, the next step is very important—you will complete a checkpoint survey at the website listed below. Each question will help inform your action plan. You will also receive a personalized follow-up via phone, email or zoom (your preferred method!) with me.**

**CHECKPOINT SURVEY:**
**www.shakethecosmos.com/checkpoint**

Thank you so much for your time, and **YOU ARE FREAKING AMAZING.**

**Shake the Cosmos!**

## NOTES | SHAKE THE COSMOS

## NOTES | SHAKE THE COSMOS

Made in the USA
Middletown, DE
04 May 2024